IT'S TIME TO LEARN CATFISH

It's Time to Learn Catfish

Walter the Educator

Silent King Books
A WhichHead Entertainment Imprint

Copyright © 2025 by Walter the Educator

All rights reserved. No part of this book may be reproduced in any manner whatsoever without written per- mission except in the case of brief quotations embodied in critical articles and reviews.

First Printing, 2024

Disclaimer

This book is a literary work; the story is not about specific persons, locations, situations, and/or circumstances unless mentioned in a historical context. Any resemblance to real persons, locations, situations, and/or circumstances is coincidental. This book is for entertainment and informational purposes only. The author and publisher offer this information without warranties expressed or implied. No matter the grounds, neither the author nor the publisher will be accountable for any losses, injuries, or other damages caused by the reader's use of this book. The use of this book acknowledges an understanding and acceptance of this disclaimer.

It's Time to Learn Catfish is a collectible early learning book by Walter the Educator suitable for all ages belonging to Walter the Educator's Time to Eat Book Series. Collect more books at WaltertheEducator.com

USE THE EXTRA SPACE TO TAKE NOTES AND DOCUMENT YOUR MEMORIES

CATFISH

Down in the river, deep and wide,

It's Time to Learn about

Catfish

A clever catfish likes to hide.

With whiskers long and smooth as silk,

It swims through waters green as milk.

Its name is "catfish", do you know why?

Look at those whiskers waving high!

Like kitty's whiskers, soft and neat,

They help it search for food to eat.

The catfish doesn't have sharp teeth,

It sucks up food from down beneath.

Worms and plants and tiny bugs,

It gobbles up with gentle tugs.

Some catfish grow both big and tall,

While others stay so very small.

From ponds and lakes to rivers deep,

In muddy waters, they love to creep.

It's Time to Learn about
Catfish

No shiny scales like other fish,

Just smooth, bare skin, so soft to swish.

Some catfish even have a knack,

For breathing air if water lacks!

Their eyes are small, but do not fear,

Those whiskers help them see and hear!

They taste the water, sniff around,

And find their food down on the ground.

Some catfish glow, some have spots,

Some are blue, and some have dots!

From golden brown to silvery bright,

They come in colors dark and light.

They wiggle, wiggle in the sand,

With fins that help them swim so grand.

But watch out, some have little spines,

It's Time to Learn about
Catfish

That poke when danger shows its signs!

The catfish is a friendly sort,

It doesn't play, it won't cavort.

But slowly, surely, it will go,

Through waters deep and currents slow.

So now you know this fish so fine,

With whiskers long like fishing line.

Next time you see one, wave and say,

It's Time to Learn about
Catfish

"Hello, Catfish! Have a nice day!"

ABOUT THE CREATOR

Walter the Educator is one of the pseudonyms for Walter Anderson. Formally educated in Chemistry, Business, and Education, he is an educator, an author, a diverse entrepreneur, and he is the son of a disabled war veteran. "Walter the Educator" shares his time between educating and creating. He holds interests and owns several creative projects that entertain, enlighten, enhance, and educate, hoping to inspire and motivate you. Follow, find new works, and stay up to date with Walter the Educator™

at WaltertheEducator.com

www.ingramcontent.com/pod-product-compliance
Lightning Source LLC
LaVergne TN
LVHW051919060526
838201LV00060B/4085